Author's Acknowledgments

Thanks to my brother Bill Barzelay for starting me on this journey. Thanks too to the Muskrat Writing Group, among them Jane Resh Thomas, Kristin Gallagher, and Laurie Richardson Johnson, for helping guide the writing process. To all who organized and sponsored the traveling exhibit Kindertransport—Rescuing Children on the Brink of War created by Yeshiva University Museum and the Leo Baeck Institute at the Center for Jewish History and hosted by the American Swedish Institute of Minneapolis, thank you for making the exhibit's extensive research and lectures available to the public. Heartfelt gratitude also to Professor Emeritus of History Gary B. Cohen, University of Minnesota, and Professor Emerita Michal Moskow, Metropolitan State University, for their thorough historical review of this work, and to Nick Winton, son of Sir Nicholas Winton, for his generous time and helpful review of this story. Agent Rubin Pfeffer, editor Carol Hinz, art director Danielle Carnito, and illustrator Selina Alko, my hand is over my heart. Lastly, I am forever grateful to my husband, Kim Stelson.

Carolrhoda Books®
An imprint of Lerner Publishing Group, Inc.
241 First Avenue North
Minneapolis, MN 55401 USA

For reading levels and more information, look up this title at www.lernerbooks.com.

Back matter photo credits: Yad Vashem, p. 37; John Stillwell/Alamy Stock Photo, p. 38 (top); AP Photo/CTK/Stan Peska, p. 38 (center); Chris Jackson/Getty Images, p. 38 (bottom); AP Photo/Tara Todras-Whitehill, p. 39.

Designed by Danielle Carnito.
Main body text set in ITC Avant Garde Gothic Std.
Typeface provided by International Typeface Corporation.
The illustrations in this book were created with acrylic paint, colored pencil, and collage.

Library of Congress Cataloging-in-Publication Data

Names: Stelson, Caren, 1951- author. | Alko, Selina, illustrator.
Title: Stars of the night : the courageous children of the Czech Kindertransport / Caren Stelson ; illustrated by Selina Alko
Other titles: Courageous children of the Czech Kindertransport /
Description: Minneapolis : Carolrhoda Books, [2023] | Includes bibliographical references. | Audience: Ages 7–11 | Audience: Grades 2–3 | Summary: "The powerful and sensitively told true story of the Czech Kindertransport, which rescued 669 children from Nazi persecution on the eve of World War II" —Provided by publisher.
Identifiers: LCCN 2022023563 (print) | LCCN 2022023564 (ebook) | ISBN 9781541598683 (library binding) | ISBN 9781728479255 (ebook)
Subjects: LCSH: Kindertransports (Rescue operations)—Czech Republic—Juvenile literature. | World War, 1939-1945—Jews—Rescue—Great Britain—Juvenile literature. | Holocaust, Jewish (1939-1945)—Czech Republic—Prague—Juvenile literature. | Jewish children—Czech Republic—Juvenile literature. | Jewish refugees—Great Britain—Juvenile literature. | Jewish children—Great Britain—Juvenile literature.
Classification: LCC D804.6 .S74 2023 (print) | LCC D804.6 (ebook) | DDC 940.53/18083—dc23/eng/20220520

LC record available at https://lccn.loc.gov/2022023563
LC ebook record available at https://lccn.loc.gov/2022023564

Stars of the Night

The
Courageous
Children
of the
Czech Kindertransport

CAREN STELSON

Illustrations by
SELINA ALKO

Carolrhoda Books
Minneapolis

Dedicated to every child in need of safe passage
and a ticket to life—
and to Reid and Lucy
—C.S.

For my beloved kinder, Isaiah and Ginger
—S.A.

Czechoslovakia
1938

When we were seven or eight or nine or ten, our home was the old city of Prague.

In the summer when the sun lit up the sky, our mothers brought us to the city parks.

We counted the boats on the river and had picnics of dark bread with cheese and slices of our mothers' sweet honey cake.

In the winter, we skated on the rivers until the first stars appeared. Then we walked hand in hand with our fathers to the coffeehouses. Our fathers sipped from steaming cups. We slurped hot cocoa and buried our noses in whipped cream.

All through the year, we played with our friends, went to school
with them, laughed and told our secrets to them. We were Jewish.
They were often not.

It didn't matter to us.

When we were seven or eight or nine or ten,
Prague was everyone's peaceful home,
until it wasn't.

In November, something happened, but we didn't understand what it was.

Tent camps grew outside our city, filled with people our parents called *refugees*.
The children appeared in the streets, cold, hungry, without shoes.
They looked lost. Afraid. What had happened to them?

We began to understand.

In Germany, Jewish storefronts had been smashed. Synagogues had been burned. The refugees were looking for somewhere safe to go.

As we walked home from school, older boys glared at us, their fists raised. One of them pointed and sneered, "Hey, Jew." Another boy threatened to beat us up.

hey, Jew

We ran as fast as we could into the arms of our parents.

Our mothers and fathers shuddered. Their faces were full of dread.
Our mothers were too worried to answer our questions.
Our fathers were too busy writing letters to explain.

One morning our fathers sat with our mothers at the kitchen table.
"It's decided. We will meet the man. He will make the arrangements."

Tears welled in their eyes.

Our parents left for a hotel with folders full of papers. Drawings we had made. Photos of us.

What man were they meeting in our city of Prague?

What arrangements were they making?

We did not know.

On a cold spring day in March 1939, an army of German soldiers marched into our city of Prague. Their black boots clattered on our cobblestone streets.

Hitler, their leader with a mustache, stood up in a car, one arm straight in front of him. Red flags with black zigzags hung on buildings or were hoisted up on poles. Crowds lining the streets watched silently.

We peered out our windows.

"War." The word escaped from our fathers' lips.

War?

We knew the word, but what would war mean for us?

We were soon to find out.

One day our fathers received a letter.

"It's time."

Our mothers began packing our clothes in suitcases.
They asked us which toys and books we wanted most to take.

"To where?"

"To England, my darlings." Our mothers trembled as they folded our
warmest sweaters, our favorite dresses. They slipped in family photos,
a teddy bear, writing paper, a diary.

"You're taking a holiday to England."

"Aren't you coming?"

"No, my loves. But good people
will be there to take care of you."

Our mothers wrapped their arms around us.

We smelled their perfume, the scent of their hair.

Then our mothers whispered words we would never forget:

"There will be times when you'll feel lonely and homesick. Let the stars of the night and the sun of the day be the messenger of our thoughts and love."

The day we arrived at Prague's Wilson Railway Station, the platform was filled with families, mostly Jewish. Some were refugees. Others were from the city, like us.

German soldiers with rifles surveyed the crowd. Our fathers eyed the soldiers while our mothers cupped our cheeks in their hands. They stared at us with wet eyes, memorizing our faces.

Our parents hung strings around our necks tied to white cardboard with numbers written on them. "Dear ones, this is your ticket to life."

We stood bewildered.

Our parents never told us why they were sending us away.

They never named the man who gave us our "ticket to life."

A train engine chugged into the station and squealed to a stop. Our parents gave us one last, long hug before we climbed into the train car. We opened the windows and peered out.

One mother stood on the platform clutching her little girl, hesitated, then pushed her daughter through the window to us. The conductor blew his whistle. Quickly, the mother pulled her little girl out, back into her arms. The mother's dark eyes darted to the train, to her little girl's face, to us. We stared back. We wanted to be in our mothers' arms too.

A final whistle blew. The engine huffed. The train wheels began to turn. The mother hugged her little girl one last time, then ran crying, pushing her daughter headfirst through the window into our small laps and arms.

The train lurched forward.

We stuck out our hands and waved.

Our parents waved back.

The train clattered faster. We settled into worn leather seats and looked around. The entire train car was filled with children. It didn't matter where we were from. We were all refugees now.

"We love you.
We love you.

Remember the stars
and the sun."

We shared our sandwiches of dark bread with cheese and slices of honey cake. We shared our family photos and told ourselves we would be home again soon.

It was a big adventure, until it wasn't.

At the German border, the train slowed. Stopped.

The German police stomped into our train car. We cringed and hid away our photos and our teddy bears.

The police snarled at us with angry voices. They squinted at our travel documents. They opened our suitcases and dumped out our belongings.

That's when we knew we had no idea what would happen to us. No idea what lay ahead.

Our train rattled through the heart of Germany, all the way to the Netherlands.

When we reached the English Channel, we stepped out and climbed into a big boat. As the waves rocked us, we whispered to the stars of the night. We called to the sun of the day. We pictured our parents' faces and swallowed the lumps in our throats.

After another train ride, we finally arrived at London's Liverpool Street Station. Strangers with open arms ran to greet us. They peered at the cardboard numbers around our necks. They matched our faces with photos in their hands. These strangers, our new foster mums and dads, spoke English words we could not understand.

None of us knew that a man in London had asked these families to take care of us as if we were their own.

Our foster families opened their homes to us. They fed us crispy fish and chips with mushy peas and wet, pillowy white bread. By the sun of the day, we thanked these strangers. But at night, we whispered to the stars how we missed dark bread, hot cocoa, and our mothers' sweet honey cake.

Weeks passed. Months. A year. We went to school.
Made friends. Learned English.

We huddled around the radio and listened to the news.
War had broken out, as our fathers had feared.

More years passed. Cities were bombed. And Prague? Our parks? Our coffeehouses? Our homes? We watched newsreels of people wearing yellow stars sewn to their shabby coats. German soldiers shoved these people into train cars made for cattle—trains that were traveling to terrible places. We prayed to the stars of the night and the sun of the day that these people were not our parents. Weren't our parents still safe at home in our old city of Prague?

And then, the war ended. When we were seventeen or eighteen or older, we traveled back to Prague. We searched long lists looking for our parents' names. We begged people in the parks, "Have you seen our mothers?" We visited coffeehouses. "Do you know where our fathers are?"

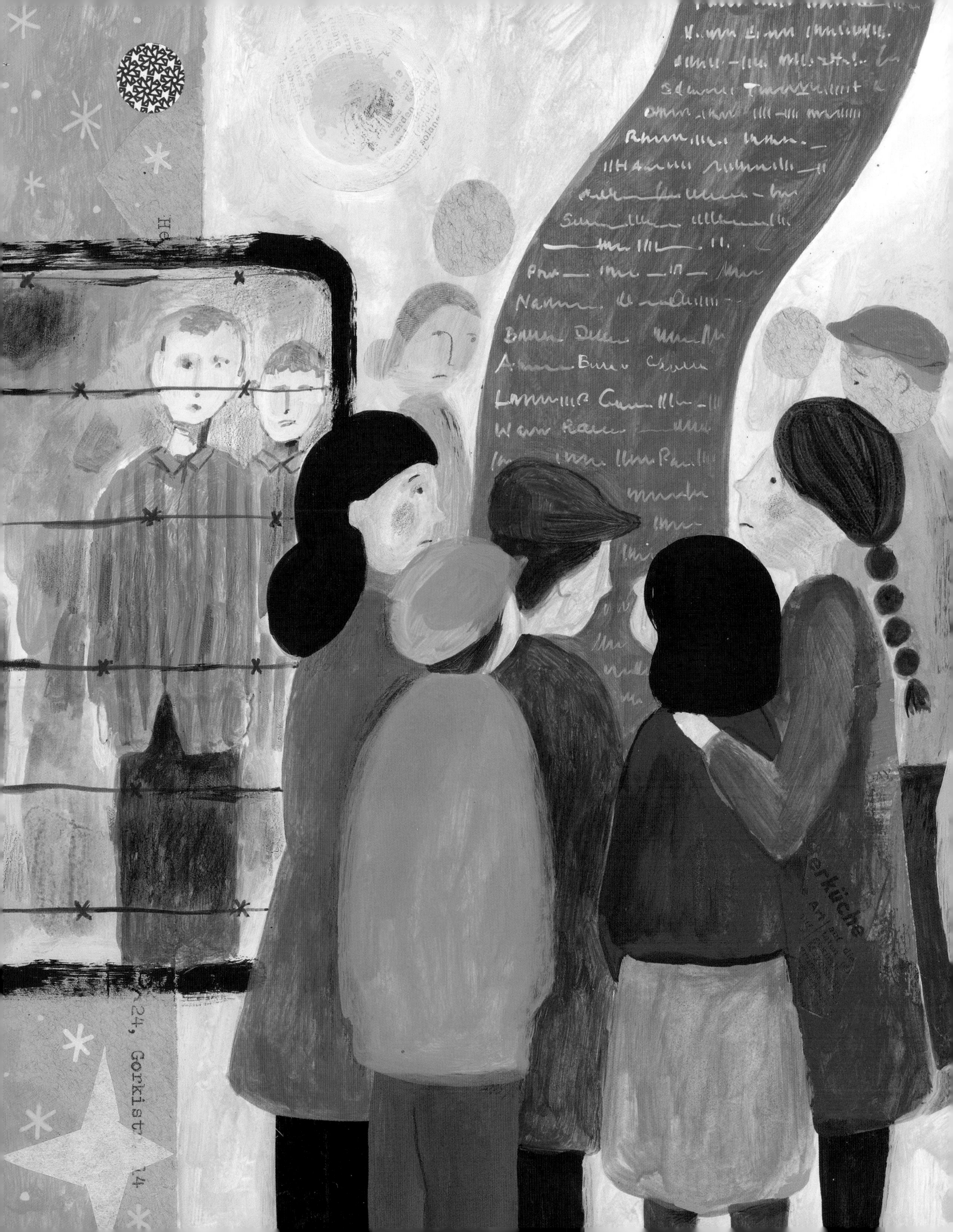

Most of us never found them, our mothers and fathers.

It was then that we understood. The worst had happened.

Our parents had been sent to those terrible places.

No one had saved our parents.

But who was the man who saved us?

Fifty years passed.

We grew up. We made new homes. We started new jobs. We found hope and courage. We had children. We had grandchildren. We whispered to the stars of the night and the sun of the day our gratitude for being alive.

Still, we did not know the name of the man who saved us—until one day.

News came that a scrapbook had been found in an old trunk in an attic. Inside the scrapbook were photos of children. Their drawings. Passports. Legal stamps. Letters. A plan of escape. And names and names listed in rows. Our photos were pasted in that scrapbook. Our names were on the lists. The name of the man who made the lists was in the scrapbook too.

Who was this man?

After all these years, we wanted to know.

One day we were invited to meet him. He was an elderly man wearing an ordinary suit, looking with kind eyes through ordinary glasses.

But he was no ordinary man.
His name was Nicholas Winton.

He was the man in Prague.
He was the man in London.
He was the man who wanted to save children.
Nicholas Winton was the man who wanted to save us.

He saved 669 of us.

We will forever whisper our thanks to him.
By saving us as children, Nicholas Winton saved our children,
our grandchildren, and all their children to come.

We will forever whisper our thanks to

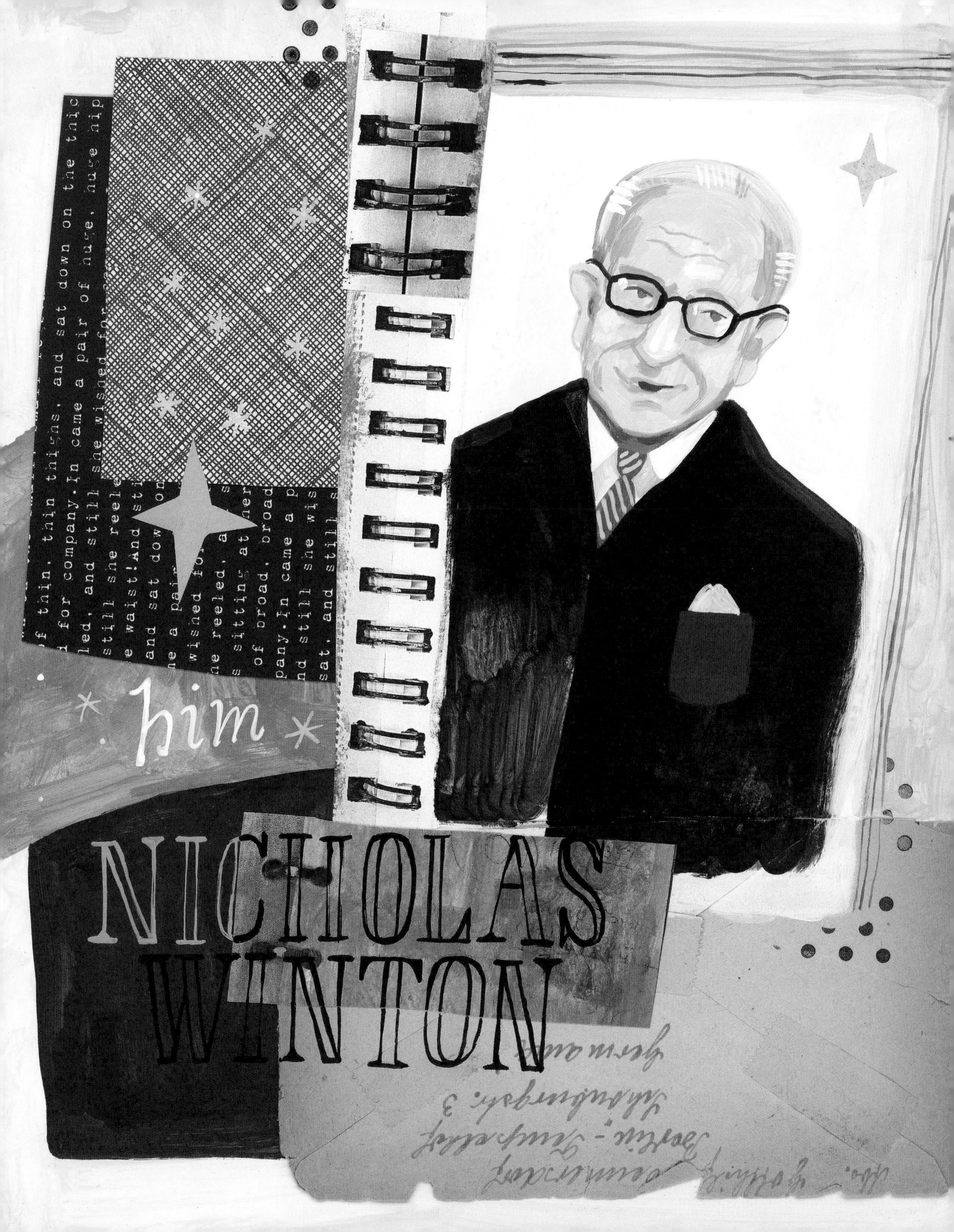
him
NICHOLAS WINTON

THE KINDERTRANSPORT MOVEMENT

The story told in *Stars of the Night* took place just before World War II (1939–1945) broke out in Europe. During the war, the German Nazi government of Adolf Hitler murdered six million Jewish people, which is known as the Holocaust. That number includes the parents of most of the children who were sent away on the Kindertransport. To fully appreciate Nicholas Winton's heroic efforts to save 669 Czechoslovakian children from the Nazis, it is helpful to understand the larger Kindertransport movement. Even before Winton began his work in Prague, humanitarian workers in Germany, Austria, and the Netherlands had begun working with refugee organizations in Britain to secure safe homes for Jewish children. In the course of nine months, from December 1938 to the outbreak of World War II, Kindertransport volunteers brought nearly ten thousand children, mostly Jewish, to Britain. Although they could not have known it at the time, the children who boarded the Kindertransports were on a journey that would save their lives.

TIMELINE

1933 Adolf Hitler and his Nazi Party come to power in Germany. Their goal is to take absolute control of the government as well as all aspects of the German society and culture. Germany had been defeated in World War I. Hitler is able to leverage the anger in the country to begin a campaign of racial hatred. The Nazis promote the unfounded notion that a race they call Aryan is superior to all others. Non-Aryans include Jewish people as well as Roma and Sinti and Black people. The government begins discriminating against Jews, removing them from positions in public offices, the arts, and education.

1935 On September 15, the Nuremberg Laws pass, stripping Jews in Germany of citizenship and other fundamental rights. These laws legalize discrimination against Jews and others deemed "undesirable."

1938 On March 12–13, Germany invades and annexes Austria, a German-speaking country, as part of the Nazi's Third Reich, or empire. Following the invasion, violence against Jews living in Austria increases.

On September 29–30, leaders of Britain, France, and Italy sign the Munich Agreement. This allows Hitler to take over the German-speaking parts of Czechoslovakia, the Sudetenland.

On November 9–10, Nazis coordinate attacks on Jewish communities throughout Germany, Austria, and areas of the Sudetenland. The attacks become known as Kristallnacht, or the "Night of the Broken Glass," because of the shards of glass that litter the streets. Jewish-owned storefronts and buildings are targeted and smashed. In addition, Jewish homes, hospitals, and schools are vandalized, and synagogues are burned to the ground. More than thirty thousand Jewish men are arrested and brought to concentration camps.

Kristallnacht is a turning point. Jews from Germany and the Sudetenland stream into refugee camps outside of Prague, Czechoslovakia, swelling their numbers to 250,000. Soon afterward, the British Parliament agrees to allow unaccompanied children under the age of seventeen from Germany and German-annexed territories to enter the country. To enter, each child has to have a guaranteed foster placement and financial payment for their return home.

On December 1, Operation Kindertransport begins when the first train departs from Berlin, Germany, with 196 children on board from a Jewish orphanage burned during Kristallnacht. The children reach Harwich, England, the next day.

In late December, Nicholas Winton gets involved. Born in London to parents from German Jewish families, Nicholas, or Nicky, was schooled in Britain and trained in banking. At twenty-nine-years old, Winton is working as a London stockbroker and plans to travel to Switzerland to ski. Shortly before the trip, his friend Martin Blake calls and says, "I have a most interesting assignment and I need your help. Don't bother bringing your skis."

Winton holds a Czech child in January 1939.

Winton meets Blake in Prague. Blake is working with Trevor Chadwick and Doreen Warriner to help adult refugees from Nazi-occupied regions to safety. Winton quickly realizes that no one is focusing on the children. He writes, "I found out that the children of refugees and other groups of people weren't being looked after. . . . The parents desperately wanted at least to get their children to safety. . . . Everybody in Prague said, 'Look, there is no organization in Prague to deal with refugee children, nobody will let the children go on their own, but if you want to have a go, have a go.'"

During his time in Prague, Winton creates his own unofficial "British Committee for Refugees from Czechoslovakia, Children's Section" and appoints himself the head.

1939 Winton returns to Britain on January 21 and continues his work. With the help of a small group of others, including his mother, Winton begins raising money and identifying foster British homes, forging documents when necessary. The number of applicants grows, reaching five thousand requests.

On March 14, the first of Winton's transports leaves Prague with twenty children on board.

On March 15, Hitler's German army invades the western half of Czechoslovakia. Czech Jewish parents become desperate to get their children to safety.

From April through August, Winton's team brings groups of children from Czechoslovakia to Britain on seven additional transports. This brings the total number of transports to eight, with a total of 669 children brought to Britain.

On September 1, the ninth Winton train is preparing to leave Prague with 250 children on board when Hitler's army invades Poland. Borders controlled by Germany are closed, and the train cannot leave. This marks the beginning of World War II in Europe. The German army continues to invade other European countries.

After the war begins, Winton does not stay in touch with the children he rescued. He serves in the Royal Air Force and returns home to a lifetime of humanitarian projects.

1945 On March 25, Prague is bombed by the United States, damaging or destroying certain sections of the city.

The war finally ends in Europe on May 7.

1948 On October 31, Winton marries Grete Gjelstrup. In the years that follow, they have three children and raise them in Maidenhead, England. Winton never mentions his role in the Kindertransport to Grete or his children.

1988 Grete finds a scrapbook in the attic. Inside is a list of children's names, photos, letters from parents, and other documents—everything from Nicholas Winton's Czech Kindertransport.

Later that same year, Winton is invited to be a guest on a popular British television show,

That's Life! Unbeknownst to Winton, the audience is made up of people who had come to Britain as children as part of the Czech Kindertransport. At last, they have a chance to meet him and thank him for saving their lives.

Winton's "children," as they called themselves, never stop thanking him for saving their lives. On one occasion, they give Winton a ring engraved with words from the Talmud, translated into English: "Save one life. Save the world." Today more than six thousand children, grandchildren and great-grandchildren of "Winton's children" live all over the world.

1998   Czech president Václav Havel formally recognizes Winton for his humanity and courage.

Sir Nicholas Winton at Buckingham Palace after being knighted for his services to humanity

2003   On March 11, Winton is knighted by Queen Elizabeth II of the United Kingdom.

2015   On July 1, Nicholas Winton dies peacefully at the age of 106.

WINTON'S CHILDREN

Throughout *Stars of the Night*, five children consistently wear orange, red, dark blue, light blue, or green. These children represent sisters Eva and Vera Diamantova (orange and red, respectively), brothers Josef and Ernest Schlesinger (dark blue and light blue, respectively), and Renata Polgar (green). While they were not all in the same place at the same time in real life, they are all real people Nicholas Winton saved and help to show the collective experiences of those rescued.

On July 20, 1939, Vera Diamantova, aged ten, and Eva Diamantova, aged fifteen, hugged their parents goodbye for the last time and boarded the Czech Kindertransport. It took them from Prague through Germany and the Netherlands, to the town of Hook of Holland. They then traveled by boat across the English Channel to Britain, eventually reaching Liverpool Street Station in London. Before Vera left, her father gave her a diary to capture her thoughts and experiences. That diary and others became the material for Vera's memoir, *Pearls of Childhood*. In it, Vera wrote the words her mother shared with her before they embarked on their journey: "There will be times when you'll feel lonely and homesick. Let the stars of the night and the sun of the day be the messenger of our thoughts and love." Those words helped guide Vera and Eva—and also guided the writing of this story. Although their parents did not survive the war, the sisters never forgot their mother's words of hope and connection. As an adult, Vera made Britain her home and later became a writer and interpreter under her married name, Vera Gissing, while her sister, Eva Hayman, moved to New Zealand and became a nurse. Eva died in 2013, and Vera died in 2022.

Vera Gissing

Josef Schlesinger was eleven years old and his younger brother, Ernest, was nine when they left their home in Bratislava, Czechoslovakia, and boarded a Winton Kindertransport. Josef remembers the night their ship crossed the English Channel. The children softly sang the Czech national anthem, "Kde domov můj?" This translates into English as "Where is my

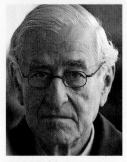

Josef Schlesinger

home?" Josef's experience in his British home was a struggle, and like most children, Josef and Ernest learned their parents did not survive the Holocaust. Fifty years later, when Josef met Nicholas Winton, Josef felt he had found a father figure he needed all along. As adults, the brothers moved to Canada. Josef became a well-known journalist. Ernest spent his career in social work. Josef died in February 2019, and Ernest died in March 2021.

Renata Polgar remembered a happy childhood in her hometown of Brno, the second-largest city in Czechoslovakia. Her parents grew worried after the events of Kristallnacht and sought a way for their only child to escape to safety. Her mother connected with a family in Britain who offered to care for her daughter. At first, Renata was excited. She would be part of the Daniels family, with a "little brother," a kitten, and a garden to make her feel at home. When the day came to travel to Prague and climb aboard a Winton Kindertransport, Renata cried. She was only eight years old, facing a journey by herself to an unknown country to meet a family she did not know. Fortunately for Renata, her seven years living with the Daniels family were full of fond memories. And out of the 669 children saved by Nicholas Winton, Renata was one of five children whose parents both survived the Holocaust. (Twenty had one parent survive.) After the war, Renata married, changed her last name to Laxova, and eventually immigrated to the United States, becoming a well-known pediatric genetic scientist. She would always remember Nicholas Winton's life philosophy, "If it's not impossible, then there must a way to do it." She died in November 2020.

STARS IN ANOTHER NIGHT: YAD VASHEM'S CHILDREN'S MEMORIAL

Although ten thousand children were saved by the Kindertransport movement, many more Jewish children did not have the opportunity to board a train to safety. Instead, they and their parents were ordered to board trains to concentration camps. Of the six million Jews murdered during the Holocaust, one and a half million were children. The Children's Memorial, part of the World Holocaust Remembrance Center, Yad Vashem, in Jerusalem, Israel, honors these youngest victims. Flickering candle flames reflected in mirrors covering the memorial's interior give the impression of an infinite blanket of stars across the night sky. *Stars of the Night* is a tribute to these children too.

The Children's Memorial at Yad Vashem

NICHOLAS WINTON'S STORY LIVES ON

Nicholas Winton's Kindertransport story is not only a story of history but also one that can inspire us to action today. In many parts of the world, children are refugees caught in dangerous situations or immigrants struggling to make a home in a new country. May Nicholas Winton's courage and forethought inspire all of us to make a difference in children's lives. To save one life *can* help save the world.

AUTHOR'S NOTE

Several years ago, my older brother Bill sent me a video clip in an email. "This might interest you," he wrote. I opened the attachment. Scenes from the now-famous BBC video of Nicholas Winton and his heroic efforts to save 669 Czechoslovakian children from Nazi persecution flashed in front of me. Until that moment, I had not heard of Nicholas Winton, nor did I know much about the Kindertransport movement. Watching bewildered children say goodbye to crying parents at a train station—I couldn't help it—tears welled up. I played the video again. And again. And again.

I began to read everything I could about Nicholas Winton, the Kindertransport movement, and the children on those trains. One morning, I woke up early and sat at my writing desk. *Stars of the Night* poured out, as if I had stepped into that time and had become a Kinder myself.

Why was I so drawn to this story?

I am from a Jewish family. We have unspoken stories about family members I have never met who died in the Holocaust. When I was younger, I read stories of the Holocaust and wondered what would have happened to me if I had been born in Europe during World War II. Which train would I have been sent on? A train to England and safety? Or a train to a dark and unknown end? After writing *Stars of the Night*, I hug my own children and grandchildren a little tighter and look for new ways to help give children, wherever they are, a ticket to life.

—Caren Stelson

ILLUSTRATOR'S NOTE

I grew up in British Columbia, Canada, in the 1970s and 1980s, an artistic child of Jewish immigrants. Although I went to a public school, my happy place was spending summers at a progressive Jewish sleepaway camp where we were schooled in the history of anti-Semitism and played capture the flag. I honed my creative skills at camp, painting peaceful murals of community and togetherness. Now as an adult, I love illustrating (and sometimes writing) children's books with social justice themes and have been doing so for more than twenty years.

When I heard about Nicholas Winton, I jumped at the chance to illustrate his story. In this case, my research meant revisiting that painful time during World War II when my Jewish ancestors in Eastern Europe were facing imminent persecution. Learning that some families were given the chance to save their children felt somewhat hopeful, and I appreciated the incredibly organized and anonymous nature of Winton's benevolent work. I began illustrating this story during the COVID-19 pandemic when children all around me (including my own) were suffering from being forced to stay at home, separated from the vital socialization that happens at school with their peers. To add more weight to the situation, as I was working on the final art, Russia had invaded Ukraine and war was raging overseas, forcing millions to flee their homes. The clear parallels around me served to emphasize the importance of getting this hopeful true story out into the world.

—Selina Alko

SOURCE NOTES

With the exception of the "stars of the night" quotation, the dialogue in the main text is based on children's accounts of the Czech Kindertransport but is not quoted directly.

"There will be times . . . our thoughts and love.": Vera Gissing, *Pearls of Childhood* (New York: St. Martin's, 1988), 35.

"I have a most interesting . . . bother bringing your skis.": "The Story," Nicholas Winton, the Power of Good, last updated May 28, 2009, http://www.powerofgood.net /story.php.

"I found out that . . . have a go.'": "The Story."

"If it's not impossible . . . way to do it.": "Holocaust Stories: In their Honor featuring Renata Laxova," YouTube video, 45:18, posted by Holocaust Education Resource Center, April 8, 2018, https://www.youtube.com /watch?v=6yKljnK23_E 22:58/45:18.

SELECTED BIBLIOGRAPHY

Craig-Norton, Jennifer. *The Kindertransport: Contesting Memory*. Bloomington: Indiana University Press, 2019.

Emanuel, Muriel, and Vera Gissing. *Nicholas Winton and the Rescued Generation: Save One Life, Save the World*. London: Vallentine Mitchell, 2002.

Gissing, Vera. *Pearls of Childhood*. New York: St. Martin's, 1988.

Kindertransport Association. https://www.kindertransport.org.

Sir Nicholas Winton. https://www.nicholaswinton.com.

"60 Minutes: Sir Nicholas Winton 'Saving the Children.'" YouTube video, 15:14. Posted by Menemsha Films, May 27, 2014. https://www.youtube.com/watch?v=c0aoifNziKQ.

United States Holocaust Memorial Museum. https://www.ushmm.org.

"Vera Gissing UNESCO 2014." USC Shoah Foundation. Accessed July 12, 2022. Recorded October 25, 1996. https://sfi.usc.edu/content/vera-gissing-unesco-2014.

Winton, Barbara. *If It's Not Impossible: The Life of Sir Nicholas Winton*. Leicester, UK: Troubador, 2014.

Yad Vashem. https://www.yadvashem.org/museum.html.

Find the complete bibliography of sources consulted at https://www.carenstelson.com.

RECOMMENDED FURTHER READING

Berne, Emma Carlson. *Escaping the Nazis on the Kindertransport*. North Mankato, MN: Capstone, 2017.

Golabek, Mona, and Lee Cohen. *The Children of Willesden Lane: A True Story of Hope and Survival during World War II*. New York: Little, Brown, 2017.

Hodge, Deborah. *Rescuing the Children: The Story of the Kindertransport*. Toronto: Tundra Books, 2012.

Hopkinson, Deborah. *We Had to Be Brave: Escaping the Nazis on the Kindertransport*. New York: Scholastic Focus, 2020.

Sís, Peter. *Nicky & Vera: A Quiet Hero of the Holocaust and the Children He Rescued*. New York: Norton Young Readers, 2021.

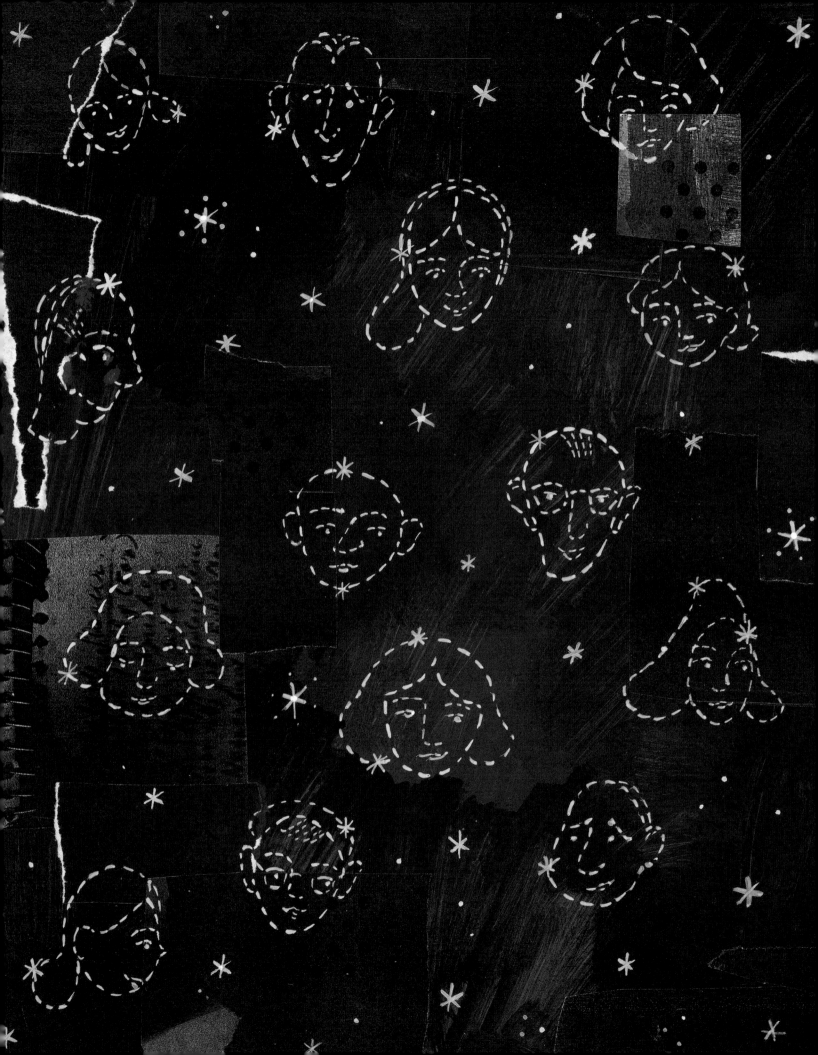